0809

LET'S WORK IT OUT™

How to deal with SECRETS

Rachel Lynette

PowerKiDS press

New York

Published in 2009 by The Rosen Publishing Group, Inc.
29 East 21st Street, New York, NY 10010

First Edition

Editor: Joanne Randolph
Book Design: Kate Laczynski
Photo Researcher: Jessica Gerweck

Photo Credits: Cover, p. 1 © Sonya Farrell/Getty Images; p. 4 © www.iStockphoto.com/Cliff Parnell; p. 6 © Martin Barraud/Getty Images; p. 8 © Emmanuel Faure/Getty Images; p. 10 Shutterstock.com; p. 12 © John Birdsall/Age Fotostock; p. 14 © Steve Satushek/Getty Images; p. 16 © Ableimages/Getty Images; p. 18 © Bruce Ayres/Getty Images; p. 20 © Uwe Krejci/Getty Images.

Library of Congress Cataloging-in-Publication Data

Lynette, Rachel.
    How to deal with secrets / Rachel Lynette. — 1st ed.
        p. cm. — (Let's work it out)
    Includes index.
    ISBN 978-1-4042-4519-8 (library binding)
    1. Children's secrets—Juvenile literature. I. Title.
    HQ784.S42L96 2009
    155.4'18—dc22

                                    2008009703

Manufactured in the United States of America

Contents

Part of the fun of having friends is having someone with whom you can share a secret. Be sure you never tell someone else's secret, though.

What Is a Secret?

Lucy and Amelia were playing catch. Amelia threw the ball and it hit the neighbor's flowerpot. The flowerpot broke. Amelia did not want to get in trouble. She asked Lucy not to tell anyone what had happened. What do you think Lucy should do?

A secret is something that you do not want other people to know. You might have a secret of your own, or you might be asked to keep someone else's secret. Sometimes a secret is just a thought or feeling. Sometimes a secret is about something that has happened or something that will happen.

Some secrets can be fun to keep and will make others happy. Knowing about or planning a surprise party can be a good secret to keep.

Good Secrets

Some secrets are good secrets. Good secrets make you and other people feel happy. A good secret does not hurt anyone.

Jason has a secret. He is making a special birthday present for his mother. Every day, Jason goes into his room and works on the present, but he does not tell his mother what he is doing. Jason's secret is a good secret. He is happy about the special present. It will make his mother happy when he gives it to her.

It is okay to keep a good secret. Have you ever kept a good secret?

Never keep a bad secret. If you or someone you know is being hurt, tell an adult right away.

Bad Secrets

Some secrets are bad secrets. Bad secrets make people feel sad, scared, or **uncomfortable**.

One day Hannah's babysitter got angry and hit Hannah's little brother. The babysitter told Hannah not to tell her parents. The babysitter was asking Hannah to keep a bad secret. You should never keep a bad secret, even if someone tells you to.

If you have a bad secret, you should tell it to someone whom you trust, such as a parent, a teacher, or a **counselor**. Telling a bad secret is the only way to get help. Telling a bad secret will make you feel better.

Some private secrets can make a person feel sad.
If you hear someone's private secret, do not tell others
or make fun of that person for it.

Private Secrets

Some secrets are not good or bad, but they are **private**. A private secret is something that you may not want to share with everyone around you. Jonah still sucks his thumb sometimes. He does not want the other kids in his class to know because he thinks they might make fun of him. Jonah's secret is a private secret.

If you have a private secret, you may want to keep it private forever, and that is okay. Sometimes it can help to tell a private secret to someone whom you know you can trust.

Mean secrets hurt other people. Before you tell or
listen to a mean secret, think about how you would
feel if someone told that secret about you.

Mean Secrets

Sometimes people tell secrets to hurt other people. Jessica was angry at Amy. She whispered mean secrets about Amy to the other kids in their class. Some of the secrets were not even true! The mean secrets spread through the class. Some of the kids believed them and started treating Amy differently. The mean secrets made Amy feel **confused**, sad, and left out.

It is not okay to tell secrets that hurt other people. If you hear a mean secret about another person, do not add to the problem by telling other people.

Telling someone your secret can be fun or make you feel better. Just make sure your friend knows not to share it with anyone else.

Telling Your Secret to Someone Else

If you have a secret, you may want to tell it to someone whom you trust. If you have a bad secret that makes you feel **upset** or unhappy, it is best to tell that secret to an adult. You should never keep a bad secret.

If you have a good secret or a private secret, you may want to tell it to a close friend. Make sure your friend knows that you expect her to keep your secret. Your friend might give you good **advice**. Sharing a secret can be fun!

You may feel angry at a friend who tells your secret. Your friend likely feels bad, too, so talking might make you both feel better.

When Someone Tells Your Secret

Dylan told Lucas that he failed the math test. Even though Dylan told Lucas not to tell anyone, Lucas told some of the other kids in their class.

Have you ever told a secret to someone who did not keep it? When someone tells your secret, you may feel hurt and angry. You may feel that this person has **betrayed** your trust. It might help to tell the person how you feel about what he did. You might decide not to tell that person another secret until you are sure he can be trusted.

If your friend tells you a bad secret, you could tell your parents about it. Your parents can help you decide whom to talk to next.

18

Other People's Secrets

Has anyone ever told you a secret? When someone tells you a secret, that person trusts you to keep it. It can be hard to keep a secret, but keeping another person's secret helps build trust.

What should you do if your friend tells you a bad secret? You can try to help your friend by **encouraging** her to tell it to an adult. You can even tell the adult together. If that does not work, you may have to tell an adult yourself. Helping your friend is more important than keeping the secret.

It is not fair to tell secrets in front of someone else. The person may think you are talking about him, or he may just feel left out.

Too Many Secrets!

Have you ever seen other kids telling secrets? When other kids tell secrets, you may feel left out. You may wonder if they are talking about you. Telling secrets can hurt other people's feelings.

If you are **tempted** to tell secrets around other people, think about how your actions might make other people feel. When you are in a group, it is best not to tell any secrets at all. If you have a secret to share with a close friend, it is best to share that secret in private.

Using Good Judgment

It can be hard to know whether or not to tell a secret. One way to help you decide is to ask yourself if telling the secret would hurt or help someone. Telling someone's private secret will hurt that person and break their trust. Telling mean secrets hurts people, too. Sometimes telling a secret is the right thing to do. Remember, you should never keep a bad secret!

If you use good **judgment**, people will learn that you can be trusted. You can be the kind of person who knows how to keep a secret and who knows when a secret must be told.

Glossary

advice (ad-VYS) An idea about how to handle a problem.

betrayed (bih-TRAYD) Turned against.

confused (kun-FYOOZD) Mixed up.

counselor (KOWN-seh-ler) Someone who talks with people about their feelings and problems and who gives advice.

encouraging (in-KUR-ij-ing) Giving someone a reason to do something.

judgment (JUJ-ment) Making good decisions.

private (PRY-vit) Keeping something to yourself.

tempted (TEMPT-ed) Felt pulled to do the wrong thing.

uncomfortable (un-KUMF-ter-bul) Feeling uneasy.

upset (up-SET) Having hurt feelings.

Index

Web Sites

Due to the changing nature of Internet links, PowerKids Press has developed an online list of Web sites related to the subject of this book. This site is updated regularly. Please use this link to access the list:
www.powerkidslinks.com/lwio/secret/